MW00723920

Share it with the one you love.

L  V E

Ariel Books

**Andrews McMeel
Publishing**

Kansas City

L ♥ V E

Debra Keller

Designed by Diane Hobbing

ISBN: 0-7407-2753-2
Library of Congress Catalog Card Number: 2002102329

L ♥  V E

Introduction

L♥ve —it thrills us,

takes ♥ur breath away, thr♥ws us f♥r a l♥♥p. It tickles us pink, makes us green with envy, s♥metimes causes the blues. T♥ be in l♥ve is t♥ be ♥n a r♥ller c♥aster ♥f exhilarating highs

L ♥ V E

and exasperating l♥ws. L♥ve, in sh♥rt, is n♥t a calm, simple em♥ti♥n. But it is a w♥nderful ♥ne like n♥ ♥ther. This little b♥♥k celebrates l♥ve and all that c♥mes al♥ng with the ride.

Even when we had no money, he never said, "Go get a job." I can't overemphasize how **important** this support was to me.

—Mary Engelbreit, on her husband's support of her artistic career

i

knew

i

L♥ved

him

when . . .

I knew I loved him when . . .

L ♥ V E

I was rounding second base, heading to third, and there he was, coaching me in the **nicest,** most encouraging w a y e v e r.

—Candace, Des Moines, Iowa

11

You talk too much,

you laugh too loud,

that's the price of

L♥VE.

—*Brian Ferry*

I'm addicted to

L ♥ VE,

just like the song!

—*Jennifer Lopez*

Every day is an anniver-
sary of something: your fifth date,
a year since your engagement,
your 3,001st day together—

L ♥ V E

celebrate it

with

I Love

Hot tips for the

romantically

```
http://www.geoc
```

L ♥ V E

challenged can be found on

Don Juan's Romantic Website

es.com/djuan80/

TRUE

L O

L ♥ V E

v e

accepts

imperfections.

How quickly bodies come to l♥ve each other, promise themselves to each other always, without asking permission from the mind!

—*Lorrie Moore*

L ♥ V E

I'd date me!

—Brad Pitt

The ten most

romantic places

to say,

"I l♥ve

you":

L ♥ V E

In bed
In public
On a train
On the beach
In a forest
In the snow
In the water
On a boat
In the rain
Under the stars

23

The most **expensive** wedding ever was that of Mohammed, son of Shaik Rashid Bin Saeed Al Maktoum, and Princess

L ♥ V E

Salama. It took place in 1981 in Dubai, United Arab Emirates, lasted seven days, and cost $44 million.

More couples are

married in June

than any other month.

The least popular

month is January.

L ♥ V E

but you can feel

L ❤ V E;
L ❤ V E

has no weight, but its

impact is enormous.

❧ 27 ❧

grow from the same kernel of

w a n t.

—*Kaye Gibbons,*
Charms for the Easy Life

L♥ve potions have been arousing passions since the dawn of civilization.

L ♥ V E

Here's a modern recipe
for **L♥ve**:

½ cup water

¼ cup red wine

a pinch of nutmeg

a bit of honey

Heat and serve warm.

LOVE is the only thing that keeps me sane.

—Sue Townsend

i

knew

i

L♥ved

her

when. . .

I knew I loved her when...

L ♥ V E

She confessed that she used to be a drummer in a punk rock band.

—*Richard, Los Angeles, California*

You know you're in

L ♥ VE when

you think his imperfections are

c h a r m i n g .

L ♥ V E

everyone

L ♥ VES

a mystery. Create your own with

a series of love notes, a trail of

sweet treats, a few little some-

things only he can use . . . sent by

a s e c r e t a d m i r e r.

37

A thunderstorm, a fallen cake, or wilted flowers on your wedding day are not omens of a bad marriage—they're just a thunderstorm, a fallen cake, and wilted flowers.

L ♥ V E

L ♥ ving

someone is a gift to

y o u r s e l f .

L♥ve

L♥VE

is endlessly fascinating,
and I never get bored by it.

—Tony Goldwyn

I saw that he viewed women as equals and treated them with respect.

—*Debbie, Plano, Texas*

Lust is the sin that gets me excited. Very excited. Luckily, because I'm married, I also get really good jewelry out of it.

—*Heather Locklear*

L ♥ V E

Ecstasy is what everyone craves—not love or sex, but a hot-blooded, soaring intensity, in which being alive is a joy and a thrill. That enravishment doesn't give meaning to life, and yet without it life seems meaningless.

—*Diane Ackerman*

i

knew

i

L♥ved

him

when . . .

I knew I loved him when . . .

L ♥ V E

He left for a week's vacation and I couldn't stop crying. He must have felt the same way because he phoned me that night to say he missed me, then he took the next bus home.

—Karen, Bethel, Connecticut

Falling in

L ♥ VE

consists merely in uncorking
the imagination and bottling
the common sense.

—Helen Rowland

Put it in writing.
Leave a trail of l♥ve
notes around the house,
car, office. Or write "I
l♥ve you" in glow-in-
the-dark stars across
the bedroom ceiling.

Being in L♥ve

a whole new spin on staying home. What you once tried to avoid suddenly becomes your dream evening.

Sprinkle rose petals

between the sheets for a

romantic

and restful sleep.

L ♥ V E

A ring from your

L ♥ VER

should only be worn on the third finger of your Left hand. It's said that the vein of that finger leads directly to your heart.

The **ups** and **downs** are crazy.

But the ups are great.

—Stephanie Courtney

L ♥ V E

If you live to be a hundred, I want to live to be a hundred minus one day, so I never have to live **without you**.

—*A. A. Milne*

i

knew

i

L♥ved

her

when . . .

I knew I loved her when . . .

L ♥ V E

♥

I tasted her cooking.

—Kevin, Ann Arbor, Michigan

Diamonds

may be a girl's best

friend but emeralds

L  V E

are the ancient symbol of

L ♥ VE,

even fleeting

L ♥ VE,

leaves you a different

L ♥ VE

person than you were

b e f o r e

L ♥ V E was

yours.

LA guy
knows
he's in

L ♥ V E

V e

when
he loses
interest in
his car for
a couple
of days.

—*Tim Allen*

63

Anticipation of *Pleasure* in itself. —Sylvia Townsend Warner is *Pleasure*

Faced with unmeasurables, people steer their way by **Magic**

—Denise Scott Brown

i

knew

i

L♥ved

him

when . . .

I knew I loved him when . . .

L ♥ V E

He made me a comic book about our relationship. It was filled with silly but meaningful details that only he and I would understand. Twenty years later, I still cherish it.

—Liz, Oswego, New York

It was the year they fell into devastating l❤ve. Neither one could do anything except think about the other, dream about the other, and wait for letters with the same impatience they felt when they answered them.

—*Gabriel Garcia Marquez*

For a little romance,
have a picnic in front of
the fire on a cold, rainy
night. For a lot of
romance,
pack the basket with
candles instead of food.

He moved across the country for me . . . and my daughter, whom he hardly even knew.

—Cyndi, Bend, Oregon

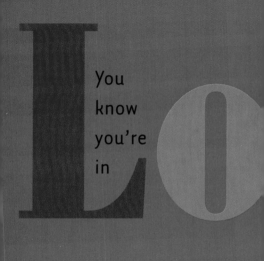

L

You
know
you're
in

O

ve

when you sing along
to songs you don't
even like.

i

knew

i

L♥ved

her

when . . .

I knew I loved her when . . .

L♥VE

She bought a flexi leash for my dog, Sadie.

—Andy, Forsetville, California

It's never too late to find

L ♥ V E

When Minnie Munroe

married Dudley Reid he

was **83** and she

was **102**.

Lazarus and Molly Rowe
were married for
eighty-six years
—the longest marriage
known.

L ♥ V E

If grass can grow through

cement, **L ♥ VE** can

find you at every time in your

l   i   f   e   .

—Cher

Set in Tarzana Narrow, **Bodoni Bold**, Eidectic omni, and Gill Sans Light

Book composition and design by snaphaus Graphics in Dumont, NJ